Unless otherwise indicated, all scripture
quotations are from the King James Version

Dedication

To the Savior of the world and the Shepherd of the Church *"...who of God is made unto us wisdom, and righteousness, and sanctification, and redemption."* (1 Corinthians 1:30b)

To the believer in Christ who has faithfully sought to lift up the downtrodden through prayer, edify the weak through God's truth, and encourage the hurting through selfless sacrifice.

Day 1- Tool of the devil

2 Corinthians 2:9-11 For to this end also did I write, that I might know the proof of you, whether ye be obedient in all things. To whom ye forgive any thing, I forgive also: for if I forgave any thing, to whom I forgave it, for your sakes forgave I it in the person of Christ; Lest satan should get an advantage of us: for we are not ignorant of his devices.

  The apostle Paul wrote the passage above because he sought for the believers at Corinth to forgive a certain brother in Christ. Many believe that this person was the same one who Paul urged the church to separate from, because of his shameful sin in having a physical relationship with his step-mother. Evidently, in time, this man became ashamed and sorrowful, repenting of his sin. Yet, instead of finding forgiveness in the church, the Corinthian believers continued to shun him.

  Thus, Paul reminded them that they were to forgive and reinstate him back into the fellowship. He then warns them of the devil's treacherous antics. The statement *"Lest satan should get an advantage of us"* literally means *That we may not be defrauded by satan.* One of the ensnaring strategies the devil uses within the church is an unforgiving attitude. The church removed the fornicator from the fellowship but invited pride and bitterness in their hearts.

They had forgotten that the purpose in church discipline was not just for the edification of the body, but for the restoration of the one who sinned. Paul revealed that if the believers would not forgive him, then he would "...*be swallowed up with overmuch sorrow* (2 Corinthians 2:7b)." Satan's goal in such a matter was to plant bitterness within the church (Hebrews 12:15) and to emotionally, spiritually, and even physically destroy the shamed individual (2 Corinthians 7:10).

Sadly, through exhibiting a disdain and bitterness, a Christian can allow himself to be used of the devil to push a fellow believer down in despair. The Church needs to be serious about the shame of sin, but also even more serious about exemplifying God's love and forgiveness. Ephesians 4:32 states, "*And be ye kind one to another, tenderhearted, forgiving one another, even as God for Christ's sake hath forgiven you.*"

For the Christian, the salvation of souls is his lifelong assignment; the power of the Spirit is his timeless aid, and the glory of God is to be his supreme aim

Day 2 – In the stillness

Psalms 46:10 Be still, and know that I am God: I will be exalted among the heathen, I will be exalted in the earth.

Much can be heard, when you are standing still simply to listen to what is around you. I recall one incident, while in a park waiting for a friend to arrive; I began to notice the sights and sounds around me more distinctly. The jumbled mass of people turned out to be different faces with specific features. The muffled noise of nature slowly became many diverse, yet unique sounds. I heard the trees rustling in the wind. I saw the children playing near the street. I heard people laughing and dogs barking. The park came alive, as I sat still simply waiting. This is because our stillness magnifies our surroundings.

In a sense, this is why God commands His children to "Be still." Oh, if Christians would only stop their busy routine for one moment and "be still" in prayer, then God would be magnified in their own hearts, as who He truly is! They would come to *know* that He is God Almighty and He *"...will be exalted among the heathen...*(and) *in the earth!"* It pains me to think of how often I treat each day as just a "routine rut" where the guy at the grocery store is just *there* to bag my groceries and his problems mean little to my life, or where I am careless about how my impatient and irritable tone comes across to the girl working at the drive through. A frenzied life can blur one's vision to where people become a common statistic rather than a cherished soul!

Do you feel like you have allowed a busy schedule to affect your testimony to man and your fellowship with God? Do the cares of this life seem to weigh you down? God's command is only to *be still* in prayer, so that you might gain a heart of understanding and compassion and not just intellectually know but experientially know that He is God.

You have two options: You can grow weary over trying to paint some perfect picture for your life by what you deem "should happen" or you can surrender to God's will, trust Him no matter what comes, and rejoice that His grace is sufficient to give you peace and strength for each day

Day 3 – Faithful through the Fire

Proverbs 20:6 *Most men will proclaim every one his own goodness: but a faithful man who can find?*

Faithfulness does not shine through convenience, but through hardships. Often it is in the tough times that we show our true colors. Over a decade ago, I helped minister at a church in Fayetteville, NC. This thriving city was home to Fort Bragg, one of the largest military bases in the world. Sadly, there were numerous times that I heard of military couples getting a divorce only a couple years after they had been married. Reasons varied, but it was not uncommon to hear similar stories of the spouse back at home being unfaithful. Time and distance, lack of communication, and separate personal struggles would devour one's devotion.

It is written, in the beginning of Exodus 15, that the Israelites sang a joyful song of victory over the power and provision of God. They praised Him, because He delivered them from Egyptian bondage. Having just passed through the Red sea, escaping Egypt, they were on cloud nine. Of course, clouds produce rain and it wouldn't be long that their hearts would become dampened. Exodus 15:22-25 states, *"Moses led Israel away from the Red Sea into the* desert of Shur. For three days they traveled in the desert without finding water. When they came to Marah, they couldn't drink the water because it tasted bitter. That's why the place was called Marah [Bitter Place]. The people complained about Moses by asking, "What are we supposed to drink?" Moses cried out to the LORD, and the LORD showed him a piece of wood. He threw it into the water, and the water became sweet. There the LORD set down laws and rules for them to live by, and there he tested them." (GWT)

After a few days of thirst, their joyous and hopeful tune quickly changed to a harmonization of depression and doubt. How is it that God parted an entire sea for them, but didn't let them have water to drink? In the last verse we read that, "*He tested them.*" God was not toying with them out of amusement or punishing them in anger, He was opening their eyes to the reality that if they were to going follow Him, trust Him, and love Him, it was going to be in the good times and the bad times. It is easy to sing praises when we watch waters part for us, but when our mouth is dry and our stomach empty, we seem to forget about God's goodness.

God wants faithful children, but to cultivate true devotion, He must bring the storms into our lives. Not so we can fail, but so we can trust in His ever guiding presence and realize that whether He calms the storm or not,

He can make us walk on water and face the raging sea with a heart of praise and love. Perhaps we need to often pray as David did, *"Examine me, O LORD, and prove me; try my reins and my heart"* (Psalms 26:2).

SUNSHINE

As the rays of the sun's effervescence

bursting forth with glory,

so Christ banished the chilling darkness

imparting life and victory.

Sunlight fills each day,

Gone are the empty endeavors.

Warm presence and grace envelops the way

May His Glory shine forth forever!

Day 4 – Get in Formation

Ephesians 6:11 Put on the whole armour of God, that ye may be able to stand against the wiles of the devil.

Throughout history, soldiers have learned formations for battle. The medieval era brought about formations like the Vanguard, which the army made the shape of a V in battle. In dire situations of defense, the Romans used the Orb formation, which was a circular position for soldiers. When the need arose, it was vital that every soldier knew how to quickly get in the right position, march in perfect line, diligently stand his ground, and fight with valor. The same goes for every believer in Christ. A Christian is a soldier of God (2 Timothy 2:3). He is in a raging battle, a spiritual warfare (Ephesians 6:12). He is to fight for the souls of men, bearing the cross of Christ in his heart, and faithfully uplift God's name in a world filled with wicked opposition.

Christian, learn your position. You are a child of God. Just as you were born of His Spirit, you are justified and empowered by His Spirit. Do not get out of the *marching line* of faith for you are called to "Walk in the Spirit," literally to get in step with God and follow His Spirit's leading. Only then can there be victory over the lusts of the flesh (Galatians 5:16). Stand firm in the faith, but never stand alone. We are to stand in the power of God (1 Corinthians 2:5). Strength to fight will never come from you. You must be "strong in the Lord, and in the power of His might (Ephesians 6:10)." It is not firepower we need, but faithful prayers (James 5:16). It is not worldly weapons that will cause the devil to flee, but God's precious Word tucked in the sheath of our hearts, ready to be wielded in any situation (Ephesians 6:17).

Finally, realize that formations in battle, for any of them to be successful, required every soldier to be in unison. Remember that all believers are co-laborers and fellow soldiers of Christ. May we never allow petty squabbles deter us from fighting in this spiritual warfare, nor be found pushing down one another in bitterness.

Every thorn of suffering that we face can become a stepping stone to Christ-likeness

Day 5 - Love Manifested

John 3:16 For God so loved the world, that he gave his only begotten Son, that whosoever believeth in him should not perish, but have everlasting life."

John 3:16 is one of the most memorized verses in the Bible. The gospel message is simplified and almost condensed into this one passage. Praise the Lord that the good news of God's love is to "whosoever believes!" What a glorious promise! Yet, even though this particular passage is well known among Christians, many do not know 1 John 3:16, which reads, *"Hereby perceive we the love of God, because He laid down His life for us: and we ought to lay down our lives for the brethren."* John 3:16 deals with God's love manifested to the world, but the later reveals the call of believers to manifest God's love to one another.

As the longest living apostle, John witnessed (And I'm sure he experienced as well) many of the sufferings and hardships that the New Testament Church went through. He also saw the divisions and carelessness that would arise within certain church bodies. In the midst of such turmoil, he wrote of the love of God and how every Christian is called to exercise a deep, pure love; foremost to God, and then to fellow believers. We need to be reminded of this today. Jesus said, *"By this shall all men know that ye are my disciples, if ye have love one to another* (John 13:35).*"* This is the true mark of a Christian! Spiritual words on bumper stickers or a T-Shirt will never set us apart. Our faithfulness to God is manifested by how we love our fellow man. We show our true colors by loving!

Notice what Paul writes to the church at Ephesus, *"I also pray that love may be the ground into which you sink your roots and on which you have your foundation. This way, with all of God's people you will be able to understand how wide, long, high, and deep his love is. You will know Christ's love, which goes far beyond any knowledge. I am praying this so that you may be completely filled with God* (Ephesians 3:17-19 / God's Word Translation).*"* If the love of God has penetrated and filled your heart, then it will surely flow into your actions. This reckless, selfless, and committed love can never be counterfeited. I may be willing to spend a few bucks on someone else, but what about spending my own life? Ultimately, we need to get back to the presence of Christ, each day drawing closer to Him. As we "plant" ourselves in His presence, His love will grow in us and overflow to those around us.

Don't let your busyness blind you of God's blessings

Day 6 – The Full Gospel

Romans 1:16 For I am not ashamed of the gospel of Christ: for it is the power of God unto salvation to every one that believeth; to the Jew first, and also to the Greek.

The gospel is the good news of salvation solely in Jesus Christ. David Livingstone, the great missionary to Africa, once said, "If a commission by an earthly king is considered an honor, how can a commission by a Heavenly King be considered a sacrifice?" Sadly, so few who claim to believe in Christ are actually committed to witnessing to others about salvation. Perhaps, one reason for this is because of a lack of understanding regarding the nature and purpose of the gospel. The apostle Paul wrote that the gospel is *"...the power of God unto salvation to every one that believes."*

Yet, many have forgotten the true reason of why Jesus died and rose again. If we're not careful, we can fall victim to the notion that the good news is simply that Jesus paid for our sins on the cross, so we can one day go to heaven. Indeed, this is only the half of it! Jesus sacrificed Himself to atone for our sins and rose from the dead that we might, through faith in Him, be given the power to daily live in victory over sin! We have been given freedom from a life of sin, not just from an eternal hell.

America is soaked with the gospel in part. Many know about the teaching of Christ's death and they also know of the teaching of heaven, but hardly anyone knows that salvation means more than just getting a free ticket ride to heaven. Salvation is for the Holy Spirit of God to live within the heart of the believer, so that He might actively work in his life and give him the power to walk in holiness. This is the full gospel!

We have become so programmed to think that as long as someone says, "I believe in Jesus to take me to heaven" that our task is done. No, certainly not. We must not finish declaring the full gospel until all realize that they have a glorious purpose here and now to live a fulfilled and meaningful life through the Spirit of Christ. Romans chapter 6, verses 12, 13, and 22 says, *"Let not sin therefore reign in your mortal body, that ye should obey it in the lusts thereof. Neither yield ye your members as instruments of unrighteousness unto sin: but yield yourselves unto God, as those that are alive from the dead, and your members as instruments of righteousness unto God...But now being made free from sin, and become servants to God, ye have your fruit unto holiness, and the end everlasting life."*

THE LOVE OF GOD

God's love can reach to the vilest soul

to the wretched, broken, lost and alone

the poor, the rich, young and old

the outcasts, the weak, the untouchables

Nothing else can redeem and transform

Scientific equations will never add to the heart

Philanthropy may nourish the stomach's cravings

But only God's love can fill the soul's longings

Psychoanalysts will never purify the mind

Only His grace and love imparted will truly satisfy

We love Him, because He first loved us

*Oh Lord, Your amazing love is my heart's rejoicing
and steadfast trust*

Let His love flow forth from your life and your lips

So that each soul reached will be eternally blessed

Day 7 – The Lost Sheep

Luke 15:4-6, "What man of you, having an hundred sheep, if he lose one of them, doth not leave the ninety and nine in the wilderness, and go after that which is lost, until he find it? And when he hath found it, he layeth it on his shoulders, rejoicing. And when he cometh home, he calleth together his friends and neighbours, saying unto them, Rejoice with me; for I have found my sheep which was lost."

This parable of Jesus, is twofold because it reveals the awesome worth of even one person's salvation and it magnifies the marvelous love of Christ. Let's look deeper into this passage to catch a glimpse of His limitless love. How did the shepherd quickly notice that one sheep out of hundred went missing? He had a *detailed* love for his sheep. He did not view the sheep as simply a numbered animal, but as a precious lamb. Each one was unique. Each one was important. Every Christian needs to ask themselves, "Do I have a love like that for others? Are people I come in contact with a valuable soul or just a simple number included in this vast world?"

Notice also that the shepherd had a *determined* love for his sheep. He went after the one that was lost. He could have thought that it was only one and time was too important to trifle with such an ignorant animal. Yet, he searched and searched to save it. I'm glad God did not leave me to myself and my wicked state, but He drew me unto Him and embraced me with open arms. Such a *resolute* love should be evident in every believer's life. Are we diligent in reaching others for Christ? Do we really believe seeking the lost and sharing the gospel really makes much of a difference?

Finally, we see that the shepherd had a *delightful* love for the sheep that was found. Oh, how it touches the heart of God, when someone embraces His Son in new life! The shepherd rejoiced in finding only one. What about you? When you hear of the conversion of someone, does your heart swell with rejoicing or is it old hat? If you truly want joy in your life, the best way is to lead another lost soul to the Marvelous Shepherd, Jesus Christ. Then you will receive delight in your heart and you will glorify God, who is worthy of all. 1 Peter 2:25 states, *"For ye were as sheep going astray; but are now returned unto the Shepherd and Bishop of your souls."*

Let's read God's Word, not out of duty or self righteous ambition, but to simply know His heart.***

Day 8 – Trust and Trials

Job 13:15 Though he slay me, yet will I trust in him: but I will maintain mine own ways before him.

The book of Job records the great faith and overwhelming trials of one man. He lost practically everything and suffered more than can be imagined. What did he suffer? Well, for starters, he lost most of his possessions and all ten of his children in one day! Not long after, Job's body was inflicted with a terrible disease, from his head to his toes, and his wife betrayed him by urging him to simply, *"Curse God and die."* Yet, in the midst of such suffering notice what Job declared, *"...The Lord gave, and the Lord hath taken away; blessed be the name of the Lord... What? Shall we receive good at the hand of God, and shall we not receive evil?"*

He understood that all he experienced, the joys, the wealth, and the pleasures, were gifts from God. They are to be thankfully enjoyed, but not thoroughly expected. Often we think we deserve the hand of blessing more than suffering and when something goes wrong, we seem to come to the point of questioning God's goodness. Yet our amazement should never be over how much we suffer, but how much God loves, is merciful to, and gives us each day. I am by no means saying it is wrong to wonder why certain things happen, but when we allow our questions to drive us away from trusting in God's goodness, bitterness and anxiety can easily control our hearts. In Psalms 73, Asaph had many questions regarding the prosperity of the wicked, yet he remained fixed on the goodness and power of God confidently declaring, "*Thou shalt guide me with thy counsel, and afterward receive me to glory* (vs. 24)."

The rain clouds may seem dark and dreary, but they are there to refresh the ground once more. Hardships should not smash our hearts, but strengthen our hope in Christ. A trial helps us know how much we truly need God. It is the prod that pushes us back to magnifying the Lord, rather than making much of ourselves. In chapter 19 of Job, he wondrously proclaims, "*For I know that my redeemer liveth...and though after my skin worms destroy this body, yet in my flesh shall I see God* (25a, 26)." His words may be several thousand years old, but they still resonate with great truth and hope.

We may not know the WHY of suffering, but we do know that the PROMISE of Life everlasting far outweighs any trial we could ever experience. Paul affirmed in Romans 8:18 that, "*...the sufferings of this present time are not worthy to be compared with the glory which shall be revealed in us.*" It is revealed that after Job's sufferings, God blesses him with greater possessions, more children, and long life. The question simply is that, in the midst of trials, do you find it easier to blame God in bitterness rather than trust Him in thankfulness? Hardships may rise like boisterous waves in your life, but remember that God is the Everlasting Rock in which we can anchor our souls.

God's Word isn't Outdated, it's Outstanding. It isn't Mythical, it's Marvelous. It is not Illogical, but Imperatively Practical. It is not Pointless, but Powerful. It isn't Anti-Science, but Anti-Sin. It's Challenging and Comforting. It's Holy and Helpful. It's a Sword to the Stubborn Sinner and Sustenance to the Seeking Saint. Praise God for His precious Word!

Day 9 – Talk and Walk

1 John 2:6 He that saith he abideth in him ought himself also so to walk, even as he walked.

The puritan William Gurnall once stated, "The Christian's life should put his minister's sermon in print." Every pastor longs for his congregation to not just *take home* what they heard, but also demonstrate it to this world. Of course, the pastor himself is held to an even greater degree of accountability. Sadly, the old adage rings true, "It is one thing to say and another thing to do."

Proverbs 20:6 declares, *"Most men will proclaim every one his own goodness: but a faithful man who can find?"* Mankind greatly struggles in this area of faithfulness and temperance. I find at times that I can easily *write off* my mistakes, yet in the same day, make much of someone else's. I seem to mentally stockpile "Get Out of Jail Free" cards for myself. But, as a Christian, I am an ambassador of Christ. I am not only a recipient, but also a representative of His grace (2 Corinthians 5:20).

Paul said in Romans 1:14, *"I am debtor both to the Greeks, and to the Barbarians; both to the wise, and to the unwise."* He knew sharing the gospel was not an option, but an obligation. Those who claim Christianity have got to realize that though they have been freed from the power of darkness (Colossians 1:13), this does not mean that they are also free from lifelong service to Christ. We have a greater responsibility; A *high calling* in Christ (Philippians 3:14). To the Christians at Ephesus, Paul wrote, *"For ye were sometimes darkness, but now are ye light in the Lord: walk as children of light...And have no fellowship with the unfruitful works of darkness, but rather reprove them...See then that ye walk circumspectly, not as fools, but as wise, Redeeming the time, because the days are evil.* (Ephesians 5:8, 11, 15-16)."

The sad reality of American Christianity is that there are many professed believers who have tossed aside church. Today, convenience rules when it comes to Christian growth. Of course, if someone is not willing to learn the Word of God and fellowship with believers, then quite certainly they are not witnessing to others as well. We must all remember that we're not playing a game, we're in spiritual warfare.

As a Christian, I am not called to simply "coast on my feelings" but I am to conquer through faith in Christ

Day 10 – Let go and Live

Matthew 16:26 For what is a man profited, if he shall gain the whole world, and lose his own soul? or what shall a man give in exchange for his soul?

It is recorded in Luke 12 of one who sought the help of Jesus in an interesting situation. He did not need healing from any physical ailment, and in a sense, his problem was not even a matter of spiritual oppression. He wanted Jesus to force his brother to give him part of his father's inheritance. In Jewish law, when the inheritance was divided among the children, the oldest got twice as much. Perhaps this person was the oldest and wanted all of the money or maybe he was the youngest and was not given any.

At any rate, Jesus simply replied, *"Man, who made me a judge or a divider over you? Take heed, and beware of covetousness: for a man's life consisteth not in the abundance of the things which he possesseth (14-15)."* Jesus had not come to settle accounting quarrels against siblings. He came to seek and to save the lost! What He told this person is something that we all must be reminded of. The quality and joy of one's life is not found in or measured by material possessions.

I have seen some families torn apart after the death of a grandparent or parent, because they allow petty squabbles over who gets the most stuff to place a wedge between their love for one other. Years ago, I spent two weeks in Moldova, which at the time was one of the poorest countries in Europe. I went to three orphanages filled with children who didn't even own one pair of shoes! Do you know what I found out about myself? I realized that my life was in great poverty. Sure I had money and I had plenty of shoes and clothes. But the eternal quality of my life was so pathetically poor that for days, when I returned to America, I was in a deep depression.

Colossians 2:2-4 states, *"Keep your mind on things above, not on worldly things. You have died, and your life is hidden with Christ in God. Christ is your life. When he appears, then you, too, will appear with him in glory."* We must remember that it is not what *we have* that counts, but what *Jesus has of us* that makes all the difference. Satisfaction can only be found through surrender. In our lives, when we are willing to let possessions and personal ambitions go, we will then see God's blessings overflow.

If Jesus lives in your heart, surely the message of His love and forgiveness should proceed out of your mouth!

Day 11 – Making Disciples

Romans 14:1 As for the one who is weak in faith, welcome him, but not to quarrel over opinions. (ESV)

How do you hammer a nail? If I were to take a nail in my hand and swing the hammer wildly onto the nail without positioning it or giving it a secure foundation, it will either fly off the surface, flipping uncontrollably to the ground, or it will get bent and may even become useless. So, it is with a young Christian. I cannot begin to hammer away my petty preferences and dislikes and expect this new believer to change into what I want. He will undoubtedly fly out of church and flip back into the world system again, or he will bend into a religious hypocrite.

Sadly, when it comes to true discipleship and edification, it is scarce within the average American church. Far too often, church leaders have sought to mold others in their own likeness, instead of living out what Paul declared in Galatians 4:19, "My little children, of whom I travail in birth again until Christ be formed in you." When teaching others, more than anything, I should seek for them to be molded in the image of Christ.

I remember when I was a young convert; there were certain spiritual guides in my life who cared more about me following a list of rules rather than simply loving Jesus. In condemning Pharisees for their hypocrisy and how they taught others, Jesus cried out, "Woe unto you, scribes and Pharisees, hypocrites! for ye compass sea and land to make one proselyte, and when he is made, ye make him twofold more the child of hell than yourselves (Matthew 23:15)."

Our holy zeal to disciple another must have the right foundation. I must first tenderly edify the young convert to make God's truth, grace, and love the foundation of his walk. I dare not hammer down my opinions and preferences, but I gently and wisely ground him into God's Word. Let us never forget to lead with love, not by a list.

A simple guide to reading God's Word is to (1) Read it prayerfully; pray for wisdom and guidance. (2) Read it persistently; make it a daily habit in your life. (3) Read it passionately; desire it and long for the understanding of God's truths. Finally, read it purposefully; in simple terms, be sure to read it to get something out of it.

Day 12 – Freedom from the Mundane

Romans 8:28 And we know that all things work together for good to them that love God, to them who are the called according to his purpose.

If you have not said it before, more than likely you have heard it at some point. Most of the time, people say this phrase when asked how their day, week, or even life is going, and instead of answering with a detailed and lengthy report, they simply reply, "Oh you know, same old, same old." I have said it before. You probably have as well. This is the way the world goes. As Solomon once said, "*The thing that hath been, it is that which shall be; and that which is done is that which shall be done: and there is no new thing under the sun....I have seen all the works that are done under the sun; and, behold, all is vanity and vexation of spirit* (Ecclesiastes 1:9, 14)."

We may expect the monotony of life, but it does not make it any easier to cope with. Indeed, some people can't shake the feeling of being trapped in never ending quicksand, while others constantly busy themselves to somehow try to push back the mundane. The writer of Ecclesiastes only looked at life through the lens of the natural man, which is what most of us do, yet for the believer, his vision should extend beyond what is in front of him. Paul said in 2 Corinthians 4:18, *"While we look not at the things which are seen, but at the things which are not seen: for the things which are seen are temporal; but the things which are not seen are eternal."* In another epistle, Paul calls Christians to, *"Set your affection on things above, not on things on the earth* (Colossians 3:2)."

There may be *nothing new* under the sun, but in God's Son there is newness of life! Our circumstances may appear dreary or painful, but because of Jesus, there is abundance (John 10:10) and purpose (Romans 8:28) in this life. Each day brings with it new opportunities to share God's love, to experience growth and spiritual transformation, and to be filled with joy and hope. Christian, life doesn't have to be the "same old, same old." It is by the surrender of the heart that we extend beyond the monotony of the world. Have faith in God's goodness, seek His presence, and be available to all that He is and all that He asks of you.

I simply ask you, what do you treasure most in your life? Jesus said in Matthew 6:21, "For where your treasure is, there will your heart be also." The more you cherish someone, the more your heart is committed to them.

Day 13 – A Rich Life

Hebrews 13:5 Let your conversation be without covetousness; and be content with such things as ye have: for he hath said, I will never leave thee, nor forsake thee.

Tucked away near the Pocono mountains, right beside a little creek, is a quaint shop that mainly sells fresh made pies and hot dogs. The food is great and the prices are too. For some it may not sound like much, but I often reminiscence about that little store, because the first time my wife and I visited it was on our honeymoon. We had lunch there and sat outside by a nearby creek bank simply enjoying life. Two years later, we took our first child to that same place, and found that little had changed. Prices were still reasonable, the food was still good, and the scenery was still serene. What's my point?

Well, the fact is that we live in such a commercially driven society that we oftentimes miss out on the little things in life that give us delight. Some people think that a family vacation has to involve going to an extravagant amusement park for several days or taking an all-inclusive cruise to a tropical island. Assuredly, these experiences can be fun, but we cannot forget that what will make more of an impact on a child is not a two minute roller coaster ride, but the time when the father plays legos with his son or when the mother lets her daughter help with preparing supper. I still remember the times when my dad would read stories to my brother, sister, and I with such creativity and imagination.

Ecclesiastes 6:9 states, *"It is better to look at what is in front of you than to go looking for what you want. Even this is pointless. It's like trying to catch the wind* (GWT)." When one is several yards away, his shadow can cast a pretty big image on a wall, but the closer he walks towards his shadow, the smaller it becomes. Constantly trying to go after *the next big thing* can yield the same fading results.

The devil seeks to keep our eyes searching for *bigger and better* things that we lose sight of the simple blessings of life. He strives to keep our focus gazing at the glittering towers of fashion and materialism that we overlook the joy found in spending quality time with family, focusing on the beauty of creation, and just simply meditating on the goodness of God. We do well to remember what Jesus said in Matthew 6:33, *"But seek ye first the kingdom of God, and his righteousness; and all these things shall be added unto you."*

The Church

Look at the stunning steeple
It is grand and high

But even greater still,
the rugged cross where He died

Look at the bright and beautiful
stained glass windows

But even more wonderful,
the cleansing blood that ever flows

Look at the large instruments
Lovely music they convey

But even more important,
The humble soul that never ceases to praise

Look at the pews, the altar,
the pulpit, and the many lights

But remember what lasts forever
the Church – believers part of the body of Christ

Day 14 – Pure Water

Proverbs 25:25 *As cold waters to a thirsty soul, so is good news from a far country*

Many people do not realize the privilege in simply having clean, cold water accessible in their home. When I fill a glass of water, to my shame, I hardly ever think about the millions of people who have died because they have no reliable source of water. Of course, in the verse above, Solomon was illustrating a bigger point than just quenching someone's physical thirst. He revealed that *good news* can be refreshing and reviving to one's soul.

Do you remember what Jesus said to the Samaritan woman by the well? He declared, "*But whosoever drinketh of the water that I shall give him shall never thirst; but the water that I shall give him shall be in him a well of water springing up into everlasting life* (John 4:14)." There are millions of lives spiritually thirsty. They are destitute of *the water of everlasting life.* They need the love and light of Jesus to quench their dry spirits and refresh their hearts.

In light of this, we must remember that Jesus has commanded every believer to preach and teach the gospel across the world. After all, gospel literally means *good news!* In essence, when we share the message of Christ, we are giving those who are spiritually thirsty a "cup of cold water" in His name. Except instead of a cup, it is more like an endless ocean of life and love! If what we have in Jesus is "...*a well of water springing up,*" how is it that it does not overflow to others?

Perhaps it is because we are like aqueducts which are useful in allowing water to flow where needed. However, the performance of such structures could be hindered by heavy debris and broken walls. In the next article, we will be studying deeper into what can "clog" the dispersion of the gospel in the believer. For now, simply remember that a heart of humility is imperative. Paul urged Timothy not to choose a young convert to be a leader within the church, "*...lest being lifted up with pride he fall into the condemnation of the devil* (1 Timothy 3:6)." When one's heart is lifted up in pride, in their lives, the pure flow of the gospel is stifled. Be a humble channel of God's love.

God is not seeking those who are strong enough to labor FOR Him, but those who are surrendered enough to trust that He, by His Spirit, will work THROUGH them.

Day 15 – A Troubled Fountain

Matthew 23:25 Woe unto you, scribes and Pharisees, hypocrites! for ye make clean the outside of the cup and of the platter, but within they are full of extortion and excess.

The last article I wrote stemmed from Proverbs 25:25 which states, *"As cold waters to a thirsty soul, so is good news from a far country."* In a way, this verse magnifies the joy and transformation the gospel can bring to a *spiritually thirsty* soul. Jesus said that within everyone who trusts Him there will be *"...a well of water springing up."* We are to be channels of the gospel allowing Christ's love to flow to this dry, desolate world.

However, lets also look at what verse 26 says of Proverbs 25, *"A righteous man falling down before the wicked is as a troubled fountain, and a corrupt spring."* The imagery given, if it was to be transferred into today's terms, is like a person who is eagerly going to take a drink from a clean water fountain, only to have someone else stick their muddy feet over the spout before they can taste a drop! If verse twenty five, speaks of restoring a heart with good news, then verse twenty six magnifies the fact that when a Christian is living a hypocritical life, it hinders the impact that the gospel can make to others.

Obviously, the whole "do as I say, but don't do as I do" mentality does not go very far. It shouldn't. Why would an avid smoker listen to an extremely obese man about how he needs to learn self control and stop smoking due to health problems? We can tell people that Jesus changes lives until we are blue in the face, but if we are not living out that *change* from day to day, the message will be "lost in translation."

Call me cynical, but I often see two camps within *supposed* Christianity. For some people, because of an ever increasing lack of biblical understanding, being a Christian simply means that you think Jesus was an upstanding guy. It is commonplace, but not trans-formative. On the other hand, I have seen people who turn Christianity into a list of rules. They pride themselves in how "godly" they look and "spiritual" they sound, but behind the scenes they indulge in shameful acts. They treat being a Christian like being on Broadway. Learn your lines, sing your best, put on a good act for everyone watching, and take a bow. When the curtain drops, you have *paid your dues* to do what you want.

The apostle Peter wrote, *"For this is the will of God, that by doing good you should put to silence the ignorance of foolish people. Live as people who are free, not using your freedom as a cover-up for evil, but living as servants of God.* (1

Peter 2:15-16 / ESV)" We must get back to the understanding that we are living letters of God's love. We are flowing fountains of His grace to this world, and when we are caught in secret sins, we muddy the gospel waters causing any kind of testimony to stagnate. Ultimately, hypocrisy begins when I live this Christian life in my own way and power. When I stop "abiding" in Christ and stop allowing His Word to penetrate my heart each day. It's not about looking MY best; it is about CHRIST LIVING THROUGH ME. Christianity only stands out because of CHRIST.

How often do many Christians think that they are doing God a favor by paying their tithes yet they reject daily fellowship with Him? How often do people think that because they have sat in a pew on Sunday, they have paid their "dues" for the rest of the week? It is not the numbers of noble deeds we outwardly do and the amount of money we give, but God is pleased with the person who is humbly available to His will day by day.

Day 16 – Coals of Fire

Matthew 5:44 But I say unto you, Love your enemies, bless them that curse you, do good to them that hate you, and pray for them which despitefully use you, and persecute you.

In the last two devotions, I have emphasized the call of witnessing and integrity as stated in Proverbs 25:25-26, *"As cold waters to a thirsty soul, so is good news from a far country* (Reflects the gospel message). *A righteous man falling down before the wicked is as a troubled fountain, and a corrupt spring* (Reveals the hindrances in hypocrisy).*"* I will now move onto the most imperative facet all Christians are to have in the midst of sharing the gospel to this world. It is found in Proverbs 25:21-22, which says, *"If thine enemy be hungry, give him bread to eat; and if he be thirsty, give him water to drink: For thou shalt heap coals of fire upon his head* (Symbolic of melting one's hardened heart with kindness), *and the LORD shall reward thee."*
It is love, plain and simple. For the Christian, compassion penetrates deeper than any intellectual debate ever could. However, the view of love in today's society is dangerously distorted. Most view it to be in direct alignment with extreme tolerance. You are to simply be a doormat for every agenda

and ideology. Taking a "stand" somehow reveals your bigotry and hatred. Shamefully, there are many professed believers who adopt this mentality of "love." Paul said of love that it *"Rejoices not in iniquity, but rejoices in the truth ."* (1 Corinthians 13:6)

It is because of God's love that we are called to stand against sin! For example, I love kids; therefore, I hate child molestation, and even bullying. God's love is without prejudice; therefore, I hate racism. Such love magnifies the sanctity of life; therefore, I hate murder, terrorism, and abortion. Ultimately, my love for God calls me to hate wickedness. To be entirely tolerant only shows that you are either too scared of others, or too self conceited to care for what's right. Jesus said in Luke 6:26, *"Woe unto you, when all men shall speak well of you! for so did their fathers to the false prophets."* Again, He says in John 15:19, *"If ye were of the world, the world would love his own: but because ye are not of the world, but I have chosen you out of the world, therefore the world hateth you."* It was once said, "To have no enemies is to have no backbone."

The reality is that as long as the world spins, there will be persecutors of Christians and ridiculers of God's Word. Yet, the gospel shines brightest into one's darkened heart, when in the midst of their criticism, I respond with gentleness and patience. It is when I am willing to help an individual change a flat tire, even if that same person, only hours before, cursed me out at work for my "foolish faith."

It is when the angry, thirsty rioters receive bottled water from the Christian company they are picketing against. It is when, the beaten and bloodied believer, somehow manages to take time to pray for the terrorists who captured him. Ultimately, such love was manifested on the cross, when Jesus cried out, *"Father, forgive them, for they know not what they do!"* We are to stand against sin, but also, in love, bow our knees over this darkened world. Shining the light starts with showing love.

———————————————

Perhaps the world crumbles, because our hearts are not humbled. Humbled to be unified with brothers and sisters in Christ, not because they wear the same "denominational name tag" as us, but because they love Jesus! Humbled to allow the Word of God to pierce through our hearts and teach us Truth and Righteousness. Humbled to not be bitter, but broken over this world! Are you ready to redeem the time by relinquishing your pride?

Day 17 – He has overcome

Hebrews 13:8 Jesus Christ is the same yesterday and today and forever.

Beginning in John 14 and continuing on to chapter 16, Jesus spoke many comforting promises and truths to the disciples. In chapter 15, He exhorted and commanded them to "abide" in Him and to "love one another." Such a powerful message was given just before Jesus would be betrayed, viciously beaten, and crucified. He was *blameless*, yet would *bear* the weight of the world's wickedness and agony on His shoulders. At the close of this message to His disciples, Jesus said, *"Behold, the hour cometh, yea, is now come, that ye shall be scattered, every man to his own, and shall leave me alone: and yet I am not alone, because the Father is with me. These things I have spoken unto you, that in me ye might have peace. In the world ye shall have tribulation: but be of good cheer; I have overcome the world (John 16:32-33)."* In pride and presumption, every disciple declared before then that he would never forsake Jesus.

However, once the time of testing came, their courage and commitment failed miserably. When the skies are blue, we often feel that we can face any storm head on, but trials have a way of revealing our true colors of trust. I find myself at times allowing even small hardships to derail my trust and commitment to God. Now understand that by no means do I want to focus on the failures of man. More than anything, what Jesus was teaching His disciples is that in the midst of our frailties, He is forever faithful! Let us look deeper as to what Jesus meant, when He said, "I have overcome the world."

You see, He reminded the disciples that in this life on earth, every person will face struggles and tribulation. Our physical bodies are subject to nature's corruption and decay. It is true that because of the sacrifice and resurrection of Christ, we can receive eternal life, but the "world" that He spoke of regards far more than just the physical. In the scriptures, satan is stated as the "god of this world" and that he has darkened the hearts of many people (1 Corinthians 4). In Ephesians 6:12, Paul reminded believers that "*...we wrestle not against flesh and blood, but against principalities, against powers, against the rulers of the darkness of this world, against spiritual wickedness in high places.*" The promise that Jesus gave was that no spiritual oppression in this world can ever overcome the child of God!

Because of Jesus, we can be victorious over temptations (1 Corinthians 10:13), we are more than conquerors in Christ (Romans 8:37), and hell itself will never overthrow the church

(Matthew 6:18)! We are free from the bondage of sin, the despair of guilt, the terror of death, and we can overcome the attacks of satan! Rest and rejoice in what the apostle John affirmed, *"Ye are of God, little children, and have overcome them: because greater is he that is in you, than he that is in the world."* Stop looking at yourself and the storm around you, and start trusting the One who is within you.

At the very outset of every day, the most imperative part is to REST IN THE FINISHED WORK OF CHRIST; to lay hold upon the reality of His abundant, overflowing grace that He so lavishly bestows upon us each day. Rest in the truth that God does not say to you "DO THIS FOR ME", but He lovingly says to you, "I WILL DO THIS THROUGH YOU." You are not called to be strong in your own abilities and understandings, but to be "strong in the power of HIS MIGHT (Ephesians 6:10)."

Day 18 – Meritorious Complex

Jeremiah 9:24 *But let him that glorieth glory in this, that he understandeth and knoweth me, that I am the LORD which exercise lovingkindness, judgment, and righteousness, in the earth: for in these things I delight, saith the LORD.*

  Several years ago, I drove a church van to pick up kids for worship services. Unfortunately, the van was hardly reliable. There were always different problems with it, yet one week in particular it kept messing up. I remember mentioning its constant plight one Sunday evening, and after the service, about 5 different guys examined it. After a few minutes, each one said they knew what was wrong with it and how to fix it. The problem was that every single assessment was different. No one would agree on the issue and each one constantly affirmed their confidence as to why they were right. It was a sight to see, because while tensions rose and egos flared, nothing was truly accomplished that night.

  For most men, they want to feel like they *know* the ins and outs of life or at least have a firm grasp on ingenuity and industry. I am always deeply bothered when asked, "What do you do all day, sit in an office?" Most do not realize that the common pastor, whether bivocational or not, averages 55-65 hours a week working. When it comes to ministry, oftentimes I catch myself "overdoing it," because I am trying to prove to others that I am not some lazy, uninformed, fried chicken eating pastor (Though I do love fried chicken).

Sadly, this "prove your worth" mindset can easily spill over into my walk with the Lord. I used to think that the gospel boiled down to me being *"saved by grace through faith"* and then I was kept secure by my own personal works. I would stick my chest out, hold my head up high, and try to assert my worth to God. I would think, *Lord, I have studied theology, I wear a tie, and I invited over 20 people last week to church! Look at how much I am worth!* In reality, I knew deep down that I was weak and empty.

It didn't matter what grand things I did or how eloquent I preached, I was not abiding in Christ. Oh, to sit at His feet and hear His heartbeat of love! This is what matters, to know Him! As Christians, we must come to the realization that there is nothing good in us except Jesus Christ and our love for Him is not grown by self righteous works, but by reflecting on His goodness and love.

The apostle John wrote, *"We love him, because He first loved us (1 John 4:19)."* We don't need to "prove our worth" because *"...God commendeth his love toward us, in that, while we were yet sinners, Christ died for us."* By the blood of Jesus, you are made whole, you are worthy. 1 Corinthians 1:30-31 states, *"But of him are ye in Christ Jesus, who of God is made unto us wisdom, and righteousness, and sanctification, and redemption: That, according as it is written, He that glorieth, let him glory in the Lord."* I serve God, not to assert my virtue, but because He is worthy of all the praise and glory.

***God is the anchor to our souls. Our faith and trust in the victory of Christ, the power of His Spirit, and the promises of His Word, is the chain that links our life's boat to God. Ultimately a thankful and rejoicing life flows from a trusting and reverencing heart.

Hebrews 13:5-6 states, "Let your conversation be without covetousness; and be content with such things as ye have (THANKFULNESS): for he hath said, I will never leave thee, nor forsake thee. So that we may boldly say, The Lord is my helper, and I will not fear what man shall do unto me (TRUST)."***

Day 19 – To tell you the truth

Psalms 5:6 You destroy those who speak lies; the LORD abhors the bloodthirsty and deceitful man. (ESV)

By monitoring the brain activity of a number of people who continually lied to their partners, researchers found that with each lie told, the amygdala which is termed as the "brains emotional processing hub" would generate less and less of an emotional response. The simple meaning is that with every lie one would tell, it became easier for them to do it again. Sadly, with some people, lying has become second nature. There are those who just don't care whether they tell the truth or not. Others try to justify their deceitfulness by either explaining it away as harmless or believing that it is essential in *getting ahead* in life.

Someone once joked, "If you trust everybody, you'll lose a lot of money, but if you trust no one, you'll lose a lot of friends!" At times, it would seem nice to have a personal lie detector on hand, but the fact is that lie detectors cannot *detect a lie.* They can only monitor ones physical response to questioning, such as the amount of perspiration and the speed of his pulse rate. There have been many who have lied on a polygraph and passed, while others who were honest, failed.

For the Christian, the apostle Paul urged, *"That ye put off concerning the former conversation the old man, which is corrupt according to the deceitful lusts; And be renewed in the spirit of your mind; And that ye put on the new man, which after God is created in righteousness and true holiness. Wherefore putting away lying, speak every man truth with his neighbour: for we are members one of another."* (Ephesians 4:22-25) No lie should ever come across a believers lips. We may say we have faith in Jesus, but He said of Himself that He is the Truth! (John 14:6) It is the devil who is called *the father of lies* (John 8:44), so if we were *honest* with ourselves, when we are deceitful to others, we are speaking the language of hell. By continually lying, no matter how we vindicate it, we do two things: We ruin any kind of godly testimony we once had and we harden our hearts to the love and will of God.

How do we maintain an honest walk? Ultimately, we must abide in Christ who is the Truth, and we must daily meditate on God's Word. David declared in Psalms 119:163, *"I hate lying; I am disgusted with it. I love Your teachings!"* (GW) When we are filled with the truths of scripture, we will realize that we are a new creation and we are called to manifest honesty in our lives. God's truth will become our guide and the light of the gospel will be on our lips.

BENEDICTION OF BLESSING

May your eyes be opened to His blessings and grace,

as you continue to seek His glorious face

May joy and peace overflow your heart,

*as you experience His boundless love the He so
freely imparts*

May you shine all the more in this dark world,

*as you realize and rest in the communion of the
Spirit of the Lord.*

Day 20 – His Power and Love

Psalms 40:5 *Many, O LORD my God, are thy wonderful works which thou hast done, and thy thoughts which are to us-ward: they cannot be reckoned up in order unto thee: if I would declare and speak of them, they are more than can be numbered.*

How often do we question the power of God? How quick are we to think that we have to do everything ourselves? The prophet Jeremiah once declared, *"Ah Lord GOD! behold, thou hast made the heaven and the earth by thy great power and stretched out arm, and there is nothing too hard for thee."* (Jeremiah 32:17) At times, it is easy to stress over finances, worry about health, and believe that many trials we face are insurmountable to overcome. Yet, in these verses, we are reminded of one truth: God is all powerful! True, there are many Christians who say they believe this, but it is only a head knowledge and the fact of God's omnipotence does not affect their hearts.

David declared in Psalm 146:5-6, *"Happy is he that hath the God of Jacob for his help, whose hope is in the LORD his God: Which made heaven, and earth, the sea, and all that therein is: which keepeth truth forever."* Peace and joy can only be found in trusting the Creator of the universe! It is certain that if God can speak the world into existence, He can sustain our lives as well! There are times that we may remember the truth that God is all powerful.

Yet, we are too prone to forget that He is also personal! Psalms 103:13 states, *"As a father shows compassion to his children, so the LORD shows compassion to those who fear him."* (ESV) We must remember and rejoice in the wonderful truth that God is not only Almighty, but also a personal, loving Father! He cares for you and me! Our trust can be strengthened so much more, when we realize and meditate over His great love for His children.

We should care more for a personal relationship with God rather than a popular reputation with man.

Day 21 - Upside Down

Acts 17:5-6 But the Jews which believed not (the gospel), *moved with envy, took unto them certain lewd fellows of the baser sort, and gathered a company, and set all the city on an uproar, and assaulted the house of Jason, and sought to bring them out to the people. And when they found them not, they drew Jason and certain brethren unto the rulers of the city, crying, These that have turned the world upside down are come hither also."*

You don't have to be a historian to know that the New Testament church was diametrically opposed to the prevalent worldviews of that day. To many of the Romans, they were viewed as disconnected with reality, strange, and even sinister. To many of the Jews, they were publicized as a thorn in society, a vile disease that had to be cured. This *disillusioned and dangerous* sect spread like wildfire. Persecution could not douse the spread of the gospel, in fact somehow suffering ignited even more flames to burn brightly for Christ. What is certain is that Christianity transforms. It stands out and goes against the current of secular thought.

It amazes me how often I hear people say that the gospel oppresses people, when history teaches that the true gospel set free those who were in bondage to the world-system. The number of Roman women who became Christians increased dramatically each day. Why is this? Because the cultural mentality of that day taught that most women were inferior and insignificant. Christianity taught submission, yes, but it also taught that women were to be loved with the same love that Christ has for His church; that they were precious to God and had a glorious purpose.

What is my point in writing all of this? It's twofold. First, I want to address the fact that the devotion and testimony of the church today is a far cry from the New Testament Church recorded in Acts. This may be obvious, but be careful not to let what is *commonplace* blur your spiritual vision and lull you into conformity. Second, I want to implore every believing heart to seek for something more, something radically different than today's norm of Christianity. We are more than just names on a membership roll, more than what has often been said, "a sinner saved by grace." We are saints (Colossians 1:12). We are more than conquerors in Christ (Romans 8:37). We are lights (Matthew 5:14). We are citizens of heaven (Ephesians 2:19). We are to be living sacrifices, transformed in our minds and surrendered in our hearts (Romans 12:1-2). Only then can we *shake the world* again for Christ.

The Saint's Song

I tried so hard for many years

My life was full of weariness and tears

I thought I had to run on the holy road

But now I see it's by resting on the Holy One

Praise God He lives in me

Praise God He set me free

Oh may I never forget

It's not through trying, but through trusting Him

Day 22 – Hurtful or Helpful

Proverbs 15:4 *A wholesome tongue is a tree of life: but perverseness therein is a breach in the spirit*

 Words are powerful. Whoever made up the song, "sticks and stones may break my bones, but words will never hurt me," had no idea what they were talking about. Sticks and stones may bruise and even break the body, but words can cut deep down to the soul. How we communicate to one another is so important. Proverbs 18:21 states, "*Death and life are in the power of the tongue: and they that love it shall eat the fruit thereof.*" What you say can bring healing to a broken heart or despair to the downtrodden.

 Over and over, God teaches us in His Word that we are to guard our tongue from speaking foolishness and filthiness. The apostle Peter wrote, "*People who want to live a full life and enjoy good days must keep their tongues from saying evil things, and their lips from speaking deceitful things .*" (1 Peter 3:10 / GWT) I'm sure you remember some time in your life hearing the statement, "If you can't say something nice, don't say anything at all." Growing up with siblings, I knew well what it was like to have to bite the tongue, simply because I didn't want to face the wrath of dad's leather belt.

Yet, as a Christian, my speech is to be governed by the love of God, not by fear. I must keep at the forefront of my mind the glorious fact that I am made new in Jesus Christ. Every believer has a new nature and a new way of communicating. Words are that much more important, because how we talk and what we talk about to others could make a profound impact in their hearts. Seek to build up and encourage lives. Share God's truth every clear opportunity you get. Speak in kindness, truth, and grace (Colossians 4:6). Romans 14:11 says, *"For it is written, As I live, saith the Lord, every knee shall bow to me, and every tongue shall confess to God."* One day everybody will confess Jesus is Lord with their mouths, but I wonder if it easy to see that Jesus is Lord of our lives in the here and now, by the things we say?

Early on children in school learn about show and tell. We do well to learn it too. Show the likeness of Christ and then you can powerfully tell others of the love of God.

Day 23 – Come to the Fountain

Jeremiah 2:13 *For my people have committed two evils; they have forsaken me the fountain of living waters, and hewed them out cisterns, broken cisterns, that can hold no water*

The prophet Jeremiah was used by God to magnify the message that Israel would find restoration, if they repented and returned to the Lord. Yet, so often, the Israelites turned their back on God and followed after many idols. In this verse, their first *evil* was in forsaking God, "the fountain of living waters" and their second *evil* was in committing idolatry. When I think of the children of Israel, I always wonder how they were so easily able to forget God. How could they reject God's provision and power and then receive pointless, powerless idols? How could they turn away from the Well that never runs dry and then seek satisfaction from the empty basin of worldliness? They traded the Solid Rock for sinking sands.

Jeremiah declared, *"Thus saith the LORD; Cursed be the man that trusteth in man, and maketh flesh his arm, and whose heart departeth from the LORD."* (Jeremiah 17:5) If they had already *"tasted the goodness of God"*, what would make them want anything else? The answer is simple: Self. They did not want to follow God's commands, but they wanted to live for themselves. Think about it. How many professed Christians do you know who are living for themselves? They work from day to day to "make a living", never considering the Lord's will in their actions. Yet, do we truly live, when we forget the *"fountain of living waters?"* Is not Christ *"the Way, the Truth, and the life,"* and did He not come to give us *"life more abundantly?"*

Invariably, when we run from the Lord's will to live out our own, we *"...hew out cisterns, broken cisterns, that can hold no water."* Our lives are practically living for something that we will never gain and for satisfaction we will never obtain. God wants to bless His people, but it must be on His terms. God wants to meet our needs, but He will not feed our sinful flesh. To me, what is even more amazing than a person running from the One who can help them the most, is the fact that God is longsuffering and His message for each rebellious heart is found in Isaiah 55:3, *"Incline your ear, and come unto me: hear, and your soul shall live; and I will make an everlasting covenant with you, even the sure mercies of David."* God is ready to receive us again into His beloved arms! We must only repent and return to be restored and receive the fountain of living waters that never runs dry. He alone will satisfy our hearts!

Fullness

In the fullness of time (Galatians 4:4),

the fullness of the Godhead was born in flesh

(Colossians 2:9), that we might receive the

fullness of His grace (John 1:16), be filled with

the fullness of God (Ephesians 3:19), and

ultimately "in the dispensation of the fullness of

times he might gather together in one all things

in Christ, both which are in heaven, and which

are on earth; even in him." (Ephesians 1:10)

Day 24 – After God's own heart

Psalms 27:14 Wait on the LORD: be of good courage, and he shall strengthen thine heart: wait, I say, on the LORD.

When God chose David to be king over His people, He said of him, *"I have found David the son of Jesse, a man after mine own heart, which shall fulfill all my will (Acts 13:22)."* We often use such terms in day to day life. For example, if a man finds out that another man has similar traits, likes, and dislikes he will often say, "Well there is a guy after my own heart!" However, what does it really mean to be one *"after God's own heart?"* To answer this, I want to focus on two factors found in the life of David.

In this devotion, let us focus on the first aspect. You see, David wrote in Psalms 62:5-6, 8, *"My soul, wait thou only upon God; for my expectation is from him. He only is my rock and my salvation: he is my defense; I shall not be moved.... Trust in him at all times; ye people, pour out your heart before him: God is a refuge for us. Selah."* Many of his Psalms reveal his spiritual longing and passion for God. Psalm 62 was written by David during a time of great distress. It is not clear whether he wrote this when he fled from Saul, or when Absalom, David's son, rebelled against him. What is certain is that even in the midst of turmoil, his hope and trust in the Lord remained. Though his outer man would flee from his oppressors, David's inner man would wait on the Lord.

This is the first characteristic of a person *after God's own heart*, to wait on God. Yet, this kind of waiting involves so much more than what we often assume. It is not about sitting idly by *twiddling our thumbs.* It is about intertwining our hearts with trust in God's word and will. Verse eight reveals two actions that are the essence of waiting on the Lord. First, we are to *"trust in Him at all times."*

There is never a time, when we should not trust in the Lord. A heart that waits is a heart that continually trusts. Second, we are to *"pour out our hearts before Him."* This is a cry deep within the soul. We must not hold back our burdens, but cast them at the feet of the Almighty. God wants us to empty our own hearts of the cares of this life, so that He might continually fill us with His goodness. He wants us to pour out our entire being, while trusting in His hand of provision and power. To, *"Arise, cry out in the night: in the beginning of the watches pour out thine heart like water before the face of the Lord...* (Lamentations 2:19)"

This is a major part of waiting on the Lord, for it prepares our hearts to gain a passion for His heart. To wait on the Lord is to daily cast all your cares upon Him, and continually trust in Him, for in Him is your *expectation*, and your very life.

Prayer is not about informing God, it is all about committing to Him! It is not, 'Lord, I want you to know about so and so' but, 'Lord, I know You know all things so I come to lay my burdens at Your feet in my own heart. I'm letting go as I rejoice in Your grace and power!*

Day 25 – After God's own heart (*continued*)

Psalms 63:1 *A Psalm of David, when he was in the wilderness of Judah. O God, thou art my God; early will I seek thee: my soul thirsteth for thee, my flesh longeth for thee in a dry and thirsty land, where no water is*

In the last article, we learned what David wrote about waiting on God in Psalms 62, which I believe is the first step to being a *person after God's own heart*. The next step is simple: It is not just to wait upon God, but also to *pursue Him*. This obviously seems like a paradox. How can one wait on the Lord, while seeking after Him? Let us look deeper into the teaching of Psalms 63.

Similar to the previous chapter, David penned this Psalm after he fled from the violent rage of Saul. Here are several key statements that he writes, *"My soul thirstest for thee, my flesh longeth for thee...Thy lovingkindness is better than life....My soul shall be satisfied....When I remember...and meditate on thee....In the shadow of thy wings will I rejoice."* David would flee for his life only to declare that the essence of abundant life is found in the Lord! He *thirsted for* and *followed after* the Lord. It is true that when David waited on the Lord, he trusted in God's hand of deliverance, and he "poured out" his complaint and burden to God.

Yet, now his waiting for deliverance and comfort is mixed with a divine pursuit for the Almighty. A longing to be satisfied not just with protection from his enemies, but with being near God's presence! Isaiah declared *"Yea, in the way of thy judgments, O LORD, have we **waited** for thee; the desire of our soul is to thy name, and to the remembrance of thee. With my soul have I desired thee in the night; yea, with my spirit within me will I **seek** thee early: for when thy judgments are in the earth, the inhabitants of the world will learn righteousness (Isaiah 26:8-9)."* His heart cry reveals that it is not only possible to wait on God, but also that in patiently waiting, the heart becomes passionate for God's ways. We transition from simple trust to a passionate pursuit, because it is in Him we are looking to for strength, and for our life's satisfaction!

*****Christ is the Lamb who was slain, so that He would become the Shepherd of our souls*****

Day 26 – Unwavering Prayer

1 John 5:14 *And this is the confidence that we have in him, that, if we ask any thing according to his will, he heareth us.*

Do you pray? Hopefully you do, but has it ever seemed that just as soon as your prayer got off the ground, it came reeling back down? Such petitions have been termed *roof requests* meaning they only go as far as the ceiling. Now if we were honest, we would have to agree that often the reason we feel this way is because our attempts to pray are flippant and few. Still, there are times when some of the most heartfelt cries seem to be barricaded by the struggles of every day life. How can we pray effectively? Ultimately, it is through the life and teachings of Christ that we find the path to powerful and meaningful prayer.

First, Jesus said in Luke 11:11-13, "*If a son shall ask bread of any of you that is a father, will he give him a stone? or if he ask a fish, will he for a fish give him a serpent? Or if he shall ask an egg, will he offer him a scorpion? If ye then, being evil, know how to give good gifts unto your children: how much more shall your heavenly Father give the Holy Spirit to them that ask him?*" So many times when we pray, we can tend to view God as One who is sitting on His throne with His hands in His ears and a sign next to Him that reads *Better luck next time.* We must open the eyes of our hearts to the glorious fact that He is our *good, loving,* and *powerful* Father; and we are His children. He loves us and longs to hear our feeble pleas. The writer of Hebrews calls believers to come *boldly* to the throne of grace. Such boldness begins with an assurance and understanding that we are God's beloved children.

Secondly, in Mark chapter 11 Jesus told the disciples that in prayer they were to *"have faith in God...doubting nothing"* (22a, 23b). Simply trust in the power and will of God. The apostle James wrote that one must *"...ask in faith, nothing wavering...For let not that man think that he shall receive any thing of the Lord. A double minded man is unstable in all his ways"* (James 1:6a, 7-8). Such wavering and double mindedness bears the picture of one coming to God with a critical and prejudged attitude.

So many times I have gotten on my knees and before my words ever leave my mouth, in my heart, I think *God probably won't answer this prayer.* It's like someone coming to you and saying, "Hey, I am going to ask you a favor, but I already know you're going to say no." They scorn your character and kindness before receiving any kind of answer. Go to God, and before you ask anything, praise Him for His goodness and the fact that He listens and will answer according to His will.

BY HIS DEATH

He was despised by righteous pretenders
Abadoned by His own followers
Betrayed with a kiss so cruel
Bartered for a guilty criminal
Rejected in His home town
Thrust with a thorny crown

Whipped till He could stand no more
Derided by scoffers and callous spectators
Nailed upon an inglorious, wooden cross
It was a moment in time, when all hope seemed lost

Yet still love and grace flowed from His lips
A dying thief would find forgiveness
In the midst of thunder and an endless dark cloud,
a shaking earth and a fearful crowd,
though some would gamble His garments away,
one Roman soldier in astonishment would proclaim
"Truly, this man was the Son of God!"
Hope began when He shed His blood

He was the Spotless Lamb, the perfect sacrifice
Through His death, He gave us eternal life
And in rising again, ascending up to glory
He gave us power, through the Spirit, to walk in
victory!

Day 27 – Humble Prayer

Isaiah 66:2b *...to this man will I look, even to him that is poor and of a contrite spirit, and trembleth at my word.*

The last devotion was about praying effectively. Sometimes it can seem that the moment our petitions come out of our mouths, they fall flat on the floor. We must understand that our feelings do not dictate whether God hears us or not, and yet, when it comes to praying, we are prone to discouragement and doubt. We need to be reminded of what Jesus taught concerning prayer. As I already wrote before, Christ showed that we are to acknowledge and be assured of the fact that God is our loving Heavenly Father (Luke 11:11-13). God cares for us and He desires that His children cry out to Him. Also, in Mark 11, Jesus said to the disciples that when they pray, they were to "*have faith in God...doubting nothing.*" Don't pray with skepticism, wondering if God really can answer your prayers. We must have assurance that no personal concern or need is too insignificant to lift up to God and we must have faith, knowing that nothing is too big for Him.

Now, let's move onto another teaching of Christ concerning prayer. In Luke 18:9-14, Jesus spoke a parable about an *outwardly pious* Pharisee and a *inwardly broken* tax collector, who were both praying in the temple. One prayed in pride, the other in humility. One left the temple with nothing, the other left with joy, peace, and eternal life. Understand that the greatest hindrance to *abounding prayer* is *arrogance and pride*. Pride creates selfish clamor within, so that one's heart cannot sense the tender voice of the Spirit. Pride blurs the mind's focus to God's glory, but brokenness bestows an openness to all that God is.

It is true that we are to *"come boldly to the throne of grace"*, but that does not mean with a sense of arrogance, as if you can control God, which is what certain foolish preachers have subtly taught. Our boldness lies in Christ's righteousness. We can be bold because He is interceding for us and His Spirit lives within our hearts, bearing witness to the fact that we are redeemed, we are saints, and we are God's children. It is hard to explain but one who goes to God in spiritual boldness and sincere brokenness manifests power and blessings beyond measure. Come with assurance in God's love. Come with faith in God's power. Come with a heart of humility and be in awe of who He is.

It is only when we faithfully face tests in our lives, that we gain a testimony

Day 28 – Baskets of Blessings

Matthew 6:25-26 Therefore I say unto you, Take no thought for your life, what ye shall eat, or what ye shall drink; nor yet for your body, what ye shall put on. Is not the life more than meat, and the body than raiment? Behold the fowls of the air: for they sow not, neither do they reap, nor gather into barns; yet your heavenly Father feedeth them. Are ye not much better than they?

At a young age, in Sunday School class, I learned about Jesus feeding five thousand people with two fish and five loaves of bread (Of course, for years, I didn't know that such a number did not include women and children so it was more than likely ten to fifteen thousand people fed!). Probably for most kids who attend church, even if it is just occasional, know about this story. Yet, there are many kids and even adults who think that such a miracle was just a one time occurrence. This is not the case! Matthew records Jesus feeding over four thousand (Again, this did not include women and children) with seven loaves of bread and a few fish.

It may seem silly but what has intrigued me most about these accounts is not the fact of how many people were fed, but how many baskets of food were taken up. There are different Greek words used to describe the size of the baskets. In John 6, when Christ fed over five thousand, there were twelve small baskets leftover. In Matthew 15, when four thousand were fed, there was seven large baskets filled with the remaining food. Why? Are these numbers significant? Is there a reason that there was extra food? Don't get me wrong, in our home we are no strangers to eating leftovers two to three times in a row!

For a long time I wondered about the baskets and prayed for understanding. Though there are a variety of viewpoints from biblical commentators, most agree that the baskets simply show how powerful Jesus is. You may say that I am just seeing something that isn't there, which is fine, but I believe that the twelve small baskets were a representation of each disciple and the seven large baskets depicted each day of the week. You see, when I muse over the numbers, I can't help but rejoice and reflect over the sufficiency of Jesus!

The baskets remind me that Jesus is sufficient for every disciple, every day of the week. He is enough! In Him alone we find abundant life that doesn't just meet the need, but spills over with blessings, peace, and joy. For every believer in Christ, there is a lavish supply of grace to empower them to walk in victory every day of the week. This is what the baskets of blessings mean to me. What about you? Are you living with the assurance that Jesus is sufficient? Do you rejoice over the wonderful truth that *"...God shall supply all your need according to his riches in glory by Christ Jesus."* (Philippians 4:19)

Leading a family begins with kneeling ---- our footprints of faith our more defined, when we pray ---- this is because a life of prayer gives us substance and weight.

Day 29 - Thankfulness

Ephesians 5:20 *Giving thanks always for all things unto God and the Father in the name of our Lord Jesus Christ*

Paul writes in 1 Thessalonians 5:18, *"In every thing give thanks: for this is the will of God in Christ Jesus concerning you."* It is undoubtedly much easier to offer up a word of praise to God, when the sun is shining and you are on the mountain top, but what about the times of pain? The times when it seems that instead of being *on top of the world*, the world is crushing you. It appears rather pointless to thank God in *everything* when everything seems to go wrong.

We must realize that thankfulness, in the midst of suffering, is vital for every Christian. Why? Because, it shifts our focus back to the Sovereign ruler and it settles our hearts in His love. You see, it is recorded in the gospel of Mark that the disciples were on a ship crossing the Sea of Galilee. A storm would come up and begin to beat down the ship until it appeared that the it would break apart. Where was Jesus during all this turmoil? Well, He was asleep near the rudder. The disciples were frantic! Almost immediately fear and anxiety filled their thoughts: *How could He sleep through this? We're all going to die! This was His idea, why would He send us straight into this storm? We don't have a prayer!* They woke up Jesus, shouting in fear, and perhaps even a little anger, *"Master, don't you care that we are going to die?"* Jesus stood up and immediately calmed the storm. He then had two questions for all of them, *"Why were you so afraid? Do you not have faith?"* (Mark 4:35-41)

Thankfulness in the midst of the storm reveals our faith in the love and power of Jesus Christ. Sure, we can question, "God don't you care?" We can shout, "You don't realize what I am going through!" Yet, praising through the pain magnifies the fact in our hearts and to others that Jesus is Who He says He is. Mark mentions that there were other little ships in the Sea at the time of the storm. Why is this important? It serves as a reminder that all of us have been through hardships. Also, all of those people in the other boats caught a glimpse of the glorious power of Jesus.

What is certain is that our thankfulness magnifies God's faithfulness and if one soul is touched by my rejoicing through suffering, then it is worth it. Don't ever forget that God cares for you, because He died for you! He can give hope in the midst of heartache, because He rose again in victory! Be thankful.

_____
Don't make today's choices become tomorrow's regrets

Day 30 – Grace to Endure

1 Samuel 17:47 ...the LORD saveth not with sword and spear: for the battle is the LORD'S

There is a specific passage that I want to hone in on which has been a starting text for many sermons. It is 2 Timothy 2:3-4, which states, *"Thou therefore endure hardness, as a good soldier of Jesus Christ. No man that warreth entangleth himself with the affairs of this life; that he may please him who hath chosen him to be a soldier."* If I could summarize every message that I have heard on these verses, it would be like this, "You better be a good soldier for the Lord! The way you can be a faithful fighter is by *enduring warfare* and not being *entangled with the world* (Gotta have some alliteration)! Why are you to be faithful? So, you can please the Master!!!" This is the gist of it and though it makes for "good" preaching , that is all it does. Of course, any preaching that only gives us half of God's truth, no matter how loud and spontaneous it may be, is of little profit.

So, what is missing in this message? We have a call to action (Endure Hardness), we have a plea for separation (Do not be Entangled), and we have a reason for dedication (To please the Father). What could have possibly been left out that is so important? Notice, what Paul urges Timothy to do in the very first verse of the same chapter, *"Thou therefore, my son, be strong in the grace that is in Christ Jesus."* This is the very foundation, the only way one can remain steadfast and set apart for God's glory. Somehow, in our personal zeal to be a good soldier, we bypass the reality of grace and our overwhelming need for it in daily life. Do not ever forget this: *Without God's grace that strengthens us, we will never be a good soldier. Grace first. Guts second.* This is imperative.

In Ephesians 6, before Paul's exhortation for believers to put on the whole armor of God, he said, *"...my brethren, be strong in the Lord, and in the power of his might (Ephesians 6:10)."* Paul went on to say in verse 13, *"...take unto you the whole armour of God, that ye may be able to withstand in the evil day, and having done all, to stand."* Truly, the first step in *standing our ground* is to be *strengthened in God.*

When fighting Goliath, David had no armor and no sword, only shepherd's clothing, a sling, and a stone. Yet, he boldly declared to Goliath, *"Thou comest to me with a sword, and with a spear, and with a shield: but I come to thee in the name of the LORD of hosts, the God of the armies of Israel, whom thou hast defied (1 Samuel 17:45)."* God's name is mightier than any Philistine numskull. Goliath did indeed end up with a "numb skull" (Sorry, but I couldn't resist)!

David was a true soldier, not because of armor or weapons, but because his faith was in God's power and his passion was for God's glory. May we start each day by reflecting on, resting in, and rejoicing over the infinite grace of Jesus Christ.

Pure thankfulness flows from a heart that has been tested in the fire of suffering and has come forth with a strengthened trust in God and a renewed desire to abide in Him.

Day 31 – Church Life

Acts 2:44-47 And all who believed were together and had all things in common. And they were selling their possessions and belongings and distributing the proceeds to all, as any had need. And day by day, attending the temple together and breaking bread in their homes, they received their food with glad and generous hearts, praising God and having favor with all the people. And the Lord added to their number day by day those who were being saved.

       Years ago, I watched an online video that was about a special "Sunday service" for professed atheists. It was called *Sunday Assembly*. The oddity of such a gathering came when I realized that almost every aspect of the service was a direct *look-alike* to the average Sunday morning worship programs held in churches across America. There was singing. In fact one of the songs was about "keeping your head up" in life. There was a special speaker who used various anecdotes to rehash the atheistic *creed* that you only live once and then death, so you are to make the most out of life. Of course, this is confusing when one realizes that the path of *making the most out of life* is always relative to a person's perception over what gives their life meaning.

Also, during the service, there was a time of giving which certain individuals would pass out a donation box. I am not at all sure why this is necessary or should be encouraged, unless it is simply for keeping up rent and electricity. The sacred principle of giving is lost in a worldview that pays homage to the teaching of *survival of the fittest.* After the meeting, several key leaders of the event ended up eating lunch at a special restaurant. This they did routinely on Sundays as well, which again mimics the same routine of church goers.   After watching this almost unheard of gathering within the circle of atheism, I began to think of how the same tune has been played for years in American churches, just with different lyrics. I then wondered, *if such "worship" can be emulated by a group that doesn't even believe in any kind of Moral Law giver, what makes "church" so special?* This was a thought that could not go away and I do not believe it is easily appeased with a quick answer.

I dare not ask an average church goer about what problems surround church; because I am sure to get the same answer that I have heard a hundred times over, "Well, this world is just getting worse and worse. That is why things look bleak for us and why the pews are not filled." Some believers foolishly maintain that the problem with the church is the world and if the world would just start acting more like the church, then the church would be able to function properly. The reality is that the status of the world has not changed. It has always been corrupt; dwelling in bondage and fear. This world-system has never been in some good/bad limbo state and then somehow made its way into lawlessness. It has always been *captive* to the will of satan (2 Timothy 2:26).

It is true that Paul said in 2 Timothy 3:13, "*But evil men and seducers shall wax worse and worse, deceiving, and being deceived,*" and he also wrote, "*This know also, that in the last days perilous times shall come (2 Timothy 3:1).*" But, many Christians fail to realize that the apostles believed the *last days* were already upon them and their generation. When speaking of the coming of Christ, Peter said that, "*(He) was manifest in these last times for you (1 Peter 1:20b),*" and again in 1 Peter 4:7, he states, "*But the end of all things is at hand: be ye therefore sober, and watch unto prayer.*" John would reveal similar thoughts by writing, "*Little children, it is the last time: and as ye have heard that antichrist shall come, even now are there many antichrists; whereby we know that it is the last time. (1 John 2:18).*"

The coming of Christ and His death and resurrection is revealed as the "fulness of time" (Galatians 4:4); however, any event after the ascension of Christ marks the *last times* or *perilous times*. The excuse that there is just too much wickedness in the world, thus causing the church to be immobilized, is a pathetic one.

So, in light of this, I go back to my previous question. If the average American church service can be easily imitated by godless individuals, what makes what we as a body of believers do when we meet together meaningful for eternity? The fact is that the true church is not rooted in programs, but in the person of Jesus Christ. After all, He is the Head of the church. Anybody can copy an order of service. They can easily mimic the tones of *worshipful* singing and even accentuate a sort of *sacred* atmosphere, but this never truly constitutes as church life. How often do you meet a soul that has been in church for years and years, and yet somehow still manages to act in spiritual infancy? I have found that most of the time it is because such a stagnant individual has placed his foundation of growth on an order of service rather than on the daily leading of the Spirit. They still have not realized that they are called *to be* the church, not just simply *go to* church. Notice what the apostle Paul once wrote concerning the purpose and function of the church, *"And He gave the apostles, the prophets, the evangelists, the shepherds and teachers, to equip the saints for the work of ministry, for building up the body of Christ, until we all attain to the unity of the faith and of the knowledge of the Son of God, to mature manhood, to*

*the measure of the stature of the fullness of Christ,
so that we may no longer be children, tossed to and
fro by the waves and carried about by every wind of
doctrine, by human cunning, by craftiness in
deceitful schemes. Rather, speaking the truth in
love, we are to grow up in every way into Him who
is the head, into Christ, from whom the whole body,
joined and held together by every joint with which it
is equipped, when each part is working properly,
makes the body grow so that it builds itself up in
love."* (Ephesians 4:11-16 / ESV)

Church life is found in the one who is
uplifting their heart in personal worship unto
the Lord without any need to be in a crowded
arena filled with people paying lip service.
They are fine with singing a song that no one
else may hear, but God alone. True church life
is about heartfelt worship and holy edification
among believers. In America, it may be rare but
believe me, this kind of *spiritual fire* is
happening all over the world. Beyond our
computer screens, our shopping malls, and our
meager church services, God's kingdom is
shining and thriving. Church life can be found
in the poorest villages and in what some would
call the darkest regions of the world. May we
all pray that the American church will
experience such a magnificent move of life and
love once more. This will make all the
difference from what is a mere service and
what is a holy awakening.

COMPLACENT CHRISTIANITY

We have our spiritual programs, concerts, and
conferences

We have mounted our doctrines, promoted our
denominations,
and pushed our preferences

We have booked calendars, busy lives, and countless
bibles

We have bumper stickers about faith, T-Shirts with
scripture, and
a mass marketed message of the gospel

Yet, there is a steep decline in church attendance, a
constant
scorn for holy living, and a growing disdain for
one's fellow man

There is confusion over identity, carelessness over
eternity, and
an increase of biblical incompetence

Perhaps it is because Christians have sought the
favor of man above the fullness of the Spirit

We have heralded our denominational differences,
rather than proclaim the gospel to all who will hear it

We mask our fear of complete surrender by hiding in a pew and handing over a tithe

We timidly wade the surface of Christ-likeness rather than willingly take the glorious dive

We must come back to a child-like wonder over God's glory and a humble heart fixed on God's love

We must heed to the words of Christ "Go ye into all the world" and rejoice in the truth that He has OVERCOME.